T0289242

People
Person

# People Person

Joanna Cho

TE HERENGA WAKA
UNIVERSITY PRESS

Te Herenga Waka University Press
Victoria University of Wellington
PO Box 600 Wellington
teherengawakapress.co.nz


First published 2022



A catalogue record is available at the National Library
of New Zealand.

ISBN 9781776920068

All illustrations by 문후경

Published with the support of a grant from

creative nz
ARTS COUNCIL OF NEW ZEALAND TOI AOTEAROA

Printed in Singapore by Markono Print Media Pte Ltd

for 엄마 / omma / Mum

# Contents

## 하나



## 둘

## 셋

# 하나

# The Magic Sock

The magic sock fitted us all—엄마, 오빠, 언니 and me. No one knew where it had come from, but we found it in the box of toys. It fit in the palm of my hand. There was only one, and it was the colour of ripe tomatoes, like my favourite snack: 엄마 sliced raw tomatoes and brown sugar sprinkled over them like dandelion seeds. We used a fork to eat the tomatoes and then passed the plate around, taking turns slurping the sweet water.

We took turns with the sock, too. We sat in a circle on the carpet in the living room. In this house we only experienced summer and everything was gold and dusty and warm. The sock was the brightest thing in the room. First, it ate up 엄마's foot, which was pale and slender. In Korea, a long, slim foot is called 칼발. She lifted that knife foot up and wiggled it around, the red nylon catching the afternoon light. Then us kids tried it on, from oldest to youngest: 오빠, 언니, then me. How could one tiny sock fit us all? It was magic.

One day, when the others were off doing their own thing, I went to try the sock on. I touched its shimmery skin and parted the lips. Suddenly the sock whispered, 'Eunsun, what do you want?' I jumped a little and rose onto my tippy toes. I glanced around the room, making sure no one was there, and whispered back, 'Can you make me loved by everyone?' And then I knew what to do. I put my right foot into the sock.

Later, 엄마 went to the kitchen to prepare an afternoon snack. I smiled my broadest smile and she picked me up from the wooden bowl. She popped me down on the chopping board, brought out a knife and began slicing me from one side to the other. Then she spread me out on a plate and began showering me in sugar. The crystals scattered onto my face, pooled into my ears. I lay there smiling, shaking my head to gather all the sugar I could.

## The Gift

In first year I liked a band called DIANA,

capitalised like that

and every time I introduced them to someone, I had to type
'diana band' on YouTube.

Sometimes, it's like that.

When I was seven, I had a crush on a boy whose full name
was longer than the English alphabet. He had no middle parting
and two middle names. They sat next to each other, like he and I
on the green bench, eating lunch, getting along.

I liked him at eight, and nine, too.

Sometimes, it's like that.

I have no middle name, but two first names.
Sometimes I hold the door and let my first name go ahead
and at other times, my surname deserves it more.

So sometimes, it's like that, too.

If I decide to give birth, I will write a list of potential names
and ask my partner to cross out any they've had a thing with.

It is quite likely that our children will not have hot people names.

Our parents bought our names from fortune-tellers,
each of the three syllables laying out our ancestry and personal truths
in the immortal wind

our names are gifts and expectations

but our English names were picked hastily
while flicking through TV channels.

Some people have an 'English name' and a 'legal name'.
They forget which names they have given to which institutions,
use one for ordering takeaways,
and for making friends.

Once, a bouncer looked at my ID, laughed and said
*Ching Chong China . . .*

Once, I applied for labouring work and they texted back
*Jo, are you male or female . . .*

Once, a little girl was introduced to the class . . .

Once, I was a lotus, pirouetting in the spring air . . .

Once, I was 조은선 . . .

# Dig Deep!

I have to write a poem
but I'm finding it quite hard
so I call him and he says,
'Dig deep!'

He is driving back from basketball
in Palmy, where he trains three times a week.

Picture him, drinking
a large bottle of protein shake
in an old Corolla, on the open road
at night.

I say, 'I just wanted to run some ideas by you'
and he says, 'You know Jo, it's a game of inches'
and I go, 'Huh?'

I proceed: 'I'm not sure if the voice is mine' and he says,
'Trust in the process. It's a long game, you've got
plenty of time' so I go,
'Yeah but musically it's not working' and

he adds, 'Have you been studying the
plays Coach sent us?' and I hold the phone
a little away from my ear,
look at it disbelievingly, then place it back.

I try again: 'Do you think writing about making dumplings
in conjunction with an inability to communicate well
is a cliché?'
He is excited now. 'Hard work beats talent when talent doesn't work hard!'

I say, 'I *am* working hard! I just need someone
to talk to'
and he says, 'Find your second wind, Jo. Are you getting
enough electrolytes?

You can't get by on just fitness, not at this level, it's about practice,
there's not much more to it.'

I wonder if he knows
who he's talking to, so I say,
'Er'
but he shouts, 'No pain, no gain!'

I say, 'Please! The pantoum is too mathematical!'
but he just goes, 'Ooosh, bro, take it easy, it's a marathon, not a sprint.'

There is a moment of silence, only
the sound of the car rushing on
like water.

I try again. 'Okay, listen—'
but he interrupts. 'The best defence is a good offence. What's your strategy?'
I look around the room we share.

My lack of response must have made him realise something because
softly now, he says, 'Jo, we got you. You got this. You're my MVP.'

This does not inspire me.
I go to hang up, but suddenly, with renewed gusto, he goes,
'Teamwork makes the dream work!'

## Send to Robyn Immediately

On Thursdays I clean
for a woman who looks like Robyn. I love Robyn!
She's so sexy, in a way that I'm working on, you know, like she
is in tune with her body . . .

Robyn's dance moves
are as smooth as eye cream
even though her limbs are reckless, like jaywalking
through a six-lane motorway on a Saturday night in Seoul.

I've tried to dance like Robyn. I've writhed
on the floor, pulling an elbow to the light,
folding a knee into a fast-beating chest
but I'm much better at folding origami,

although I can only fold a swan
and when I clean, too, there is a method
and a limit to it. Sometimes I worry this habit of sanitising
seeps into other areas of my life. I am so efficient . . .

The woman I clean for pays me for three hours
but I usually finish in two. I spend the remaining time
trying to dance like Robyn, all alone in that big house,
neck rotating in the opposite direction to the waist—

a plastic capsule with a toy inside.
They say it takes 10,000 hours to master something,
and if that's true, according to my maths, it'll take me roughly
100 years to dance like Robyn.

I’m no fool. I know it’s a long commitment
and I could practise and practise and still be no good but
*still*, my body pulses and grinds—an insinkerator—
searching for the perfect routine.

# A Winning Attitude

## 1

You hate cleaning the bathroom, but when I asked
five times in a row, you did it.

But you made it sound so hard!
I heard you grunting as you wiped the mirror
with eco-friendly streak-free glass cleaner. You wore shorts,
no top, headphones on, as if on a
building site, drilling through concrete.

You sprayed and wiped all surfaces with such vigour
I thought of rock faces eroding.

What did you do in there that what takes me ten minutes
took you thirty? Why did you *heave*?

I might have figured it out last night,
when we were watching the documentary
about the 1997–98 Chicago Bulls' season,
in particular, when Michael Jordan talked repeatedly
about having a winning attitude.

When he looked directly at the camera, I felt you stiffen.
It led me to believe that if cleaning were a competition
there would be a sponge named after you.

Training would be between 7 and 9, three times a week,
with scrimmages, social league and optional training every other night.

After all, you have to give it your all
to get a shot.

You have to be consistent
to be the best.

2

Personally, I think Scottie Pippen seems like the better guy,
the way he locked himself into a seven-year contract,
getting offensively underpaid (he was the 2nd best NBA player at the time
but only the 122nd highest paid), but he did it so he could be guaranteed
security, not just for him, but his whole family—his mum, dad and 11 siblings.

And bad boy Dennis Rodman gets my blood boiling . . .

that's not to trivialise or reduce the tender and sensitive character
who overcame a difficult childhood
and struggled with mental health, only to
        emerge
on top . . .

You noticed how I stopped talking                    mid-
                                                    sentence
when he appeared on screen
with just a basketball covering his penis,
but I was in the middle of realising that you are a piece of paper,
folded into thirds . . .

The head is competitive,
the torso nurturing
and the lower half . . .
hot . . .
. . . . . . . . . . . . . . . . . . . . . .

# 정

My grandmother was annoyed with me. It was our fourth and final meeting.
*Why don't you have this quality?*

I left hurriedly, brushing away tears, unable to answer.

high-wattage heat bulb in the bathroom on a frosty morning

borrowing undies after sleeping over

smell of their linen, when you put your head under

sharing a bowl of soup with one spoon

colour of closed eyes in the summertime

woolly insides of house slippers, on a cool marble floor

using someone else's sleeve to wipe your glasses

rolling around on plush, clean carpet

hot pink, bushy flowers against the morning blue

piano melody behind two closed doors

calling, even though they didn't pick up last time

gently taking the vape from their fingers without asking

It feels like you.

It holds like you.

# You'll Thank Me for It Later

The veins on her hands have shot up overnight, like the backs of cornered cats. They are rough as the edges of torn paper.

What if they get nicked? I know that if veins are cut, you bleed to death. Preparing meals often requires knife-handling. She must stop cooking. No, there will be no fast movements nor sharp objects in this house. We'll pack all the knives and scissors and bury them in the garden. We'll chomp on apples and eat meat from the bone.

Get the Styrofoam, and the bubble wrap. Cover all corners. TV, picture frames, yes, even the mail.

We must eliminate all risk.

Good.

Bring the cotton.

Now you grab her arms and you over there, her legs.

Her legs.

# Bones

When I was nine, Mum's teeth were threatening to fall out, so Andrew and his friends tracked down our dad. They scoured the internet and found my stepbrother, coerced him to give us an address.

Andrew, Cindy and I were dropped off on a cold night. Andrew banged on the door, shouted: 'We're here!' He was good at taking charge like that. Everyone woke up, the lights came on and we stayed for nine months.

Dad lived with his partner, her two teenagers and a fluctuating number of Korean homestay students, usually 10–15, between the ages of the same numbers. Our stepmother was direct and pragmatic, the exact opposite of our mother. 'Ajumma,' we muttered bitterly—an older woman, a stranger—as she fed us, changed our sheets. 'Ajumma . . .' cursing her with the stink eye.

Lying on the top bunk, I talked to myself. Andrew lived in a sleepout in the garden and had a car and lots of friends, and Cindy had become the ringleader of the homestay kids. I could put on two voices and hold an entertaining conversation.

Dad wanted me to practise reading Korean. He handed me a book of short stories. I read the first one. A mother and daughter are very poor. The mother goes to work in the fields and the daughter goes to school. The mother packs their lunches. One day the lunchboxes get swapped accidentally. When the daughter opens the box at lunchtime she finds it has no food, just a handkerchief.

I played knucklebones instead. I was good at counting, and I liked the bright colours and sparkly swishing sounds of Korean knucklebones. They are glittery plastic shapes, sort of flowery, hexagonal. Inside are tiny flakes of metal, like a jar of scraped fillings.

As for the nights, there was the rosary a nun had given me. The small beads were hot pink, real Barbie vibes, the large beads in between a creamy pearl. I could wrap the rosary around my hand three times. This kept me safe. I wound it tight so it wouldn't slip off when I was asleep, but it was so tight the chains erupted, one by one. Out came the safety pins.

When the mantle melts, new formations are formed. The crust cools. The lava keeps flowing inside. It rises.

# Uh Oh!

I didn’t see the exit sign being painted over.

I greet the ajoshi at the local dairy and my language ties
my laces together,
throws me on the bonnet and

drives                                        . . . fast . . .

Pedestrians watch, saying, ‘That’s *so* Asian. That’s *so* cute.’

The vehicle folds into a conical party hat
and reverses onto my head, which I wasn’t prepared for,
but the people have already lined up.

Together, they are tugging on the elastic band around my chin . . .

all of our ankles are digging in.

# The Right Way

Some people think I can't do the dishes
because I don't do it their way.

They watch me squirt detergent on a sponge
and rinse plates, bowls, forks
one at a time, under a running tap.

*Cuuuaa aaah!* they rattle, leaning in close.
'You're wasting so much water!'

They rally their neighbours
and soon there is a murder of bent backs circling
me and they caw, 'You're doing it wrong! It's all wrong!'

It doesn't matter that to Koreans, I'm acing it.
I'm really fucking good at washing dishes but

the parted beaks are getting closer,
close enough to test the water pressure and temperature.

*thip*

*thip*

The rounded heads jut up in unison.
'Fill the sink and throw everything in!'

'But then the water's grubby—'

'You're doing it wrong! It's all wrong!'

Outnumbered, I comply.

The plates, bowls and forks float
in the murky water, belly up.

My hands dip into the scene,
grabbing without hope.

I am turning the dishes in grime and debris
when I notice wings soaking
flatly, barely fitting in.

Cross-eyed, a heavy beak.

Looking down, black, crackly claws.

I continue to wash the dishes,
my feathers and bones slow and clumsy.

The crows behind me whisper *Eat them.*

# I've Seen *Space Jam* But I Still Don't Get Basketball

I'm dating a basketballer.
He's also a poet, but he never writes about sports.

On the court he's blue and white,
a rip in the ocean,
froth, the meeting of, or the peaks when whisking . . .

        egg whites . . . for the cake we snack on
while hanging one-liners from the day to dry
on the horizon.

We talked about fisheries on the drive over
and how there have been many conflicts, disputes, spats between countries
over something no one owns,
and I wanted him to place his hand on my thigh
but he doesn't like being possessive
the way I do.

I take a book when I go to his games.
He finds this offensive but I don't see what the big deal is.
I still watch him

as he wipes the soles of his shoes with his hand
to remove the dirt and as he throws
the ball down the sand-coloured shine and as he jumps up high
to intercept, get in the middle, demand full attention

which wouldn't happen off the court.

                    I don't know why I'm picking at my lips . . .

A lobster will rip the muscles of its throat, claws and anus to fit
inside a new shell,
but it probably doesn't hurt and

when the siren cries like seagulls at the bay
and blue and white singlets disperse, leaving a low tide,
we see a graveyard of long taut bodies, big claws, muscular tails . . .

## Picking the Good One

I frequent a corner op shop.
They often have 100% wool items such as cardigans and pants
and I choose them all and wonder who died.
It's a shame because she had killer style
and the right proportions.

When my mate's granny Betty died, her home became an op shop
except everything was for free and I heard all the stories.
After stuffing my car with chipped goods we shared a durry by the front door
and waved to the old neighbour who was going back inside,
and I thought of her counting the years between herself and Betty,
and how strange we were smoking so blatantly.

I keep saying I'll find the card she embroidered for me that Christmas
back when my mate drove to her house to take the trash out
every Sunday for a decade, and we used to tease him . . .

but I've moved so often I don't know where half my things are,
all in op shops really,
or in other people's homes.

When I worked in retail, we were told to present three options
to the customer, giving the impression that they had a choice, but actually
only one of them was any good.

According to common psychology, the customer will become more certain
about the good one. But what if they have dumb taste
and don't pick the good one?

What if you spend your whole life not picking the good one?

## Are We There Yet?

Back when tigers smoked from long pipes, there lived the Moon family. 문. It means 'person who writes'. The parents, four children and maid lived in a hanok built from wooden bones, with straw and dirt walls, and paper sliding doors. A dried tortoise shell hung from the wall of the main room. Outside were rows of yellow corn, a clay vessel of kimchi as tall as the oldest child, and the mountains.

One day the maid was picking purple plums when she caught sight of something white. It was the shape of a teardrop, the size of her palm. Thinking it to be a misshapen and discoloured stump of ginseng, she put it in her apron pocket and decided to add it to dinner for the lady of the house—she was ill and so required a separate meal.

The maid diced the pretty thing and stirred it into the sticky juk. She took the tray of food and tea to the lady of the house, who was sitting upright in bed, the colourful quilt folded neatly over her stomach. It took only one spoonful of the rice porridge to have her retching.

She dreamt feverishly that night. The full moon beating.

Close up. White wings sweeping dark water. Wedding gown trails on black marble. They move slowly, heavily, like pushing a roundabout in an empty playground, the carousel movement of deep breathing.

Lean out. A swan with a human face, wailing, scrunched up and blotchy, yellow snot dribbling into the water.

Wide shot. The swan is in a rice bowl. Above it is a giant human hand holding chopsticks.

The baby was named Hukyung. 후경. It means 'thick marble'. Moon Hukyung; 문후경. She was the princess to everyone but her mother. There was a street between them where the shadow of power lines offered the illusion of hope, but really, they were far too loose to trapeze across.

Her mother was beautiful. Every morning and night she applied thick creams to her face, neck and decolletage. She would change several times before leaving the house, leaving a trail of clothes behind, and her kind husband would pick them up one by one, sighing, 'Just like a butterfly leaving its chrysalis.'

The family ate with silver chopsticks, which were inscribed in Hanja. Red for women, blue for men; the different characters denoting status.

Hukyung was a happy child and when she grew into a young woman she was one of the 3% of women in South Korea who attended university. She studied art. She won competitions and had good friends, and men lined up to date her. In the mirror she saw a buzzcut, red singlet, a miniskirt shipped in from America. In the evenings she sneaked out, went ice skating.

It was around this time that she began turning into a swan. It only happened at night, and it was when the moon was at its highest. It began at her fingertips and scaled back, like rubbing suede the other way. Then she was in a trance and she used her whole being—orange beak, webbed feet, wings—to paint, turning herself into new colours and shapes. The painting happened slowly, intuitively, her glassy eyes feeling textures and spaces. She painted until she fell asleep, whereupon her body turned back into a human form, her long neck curling down to her chest.

In the mornings she looked at what she'd done and saw that she was evolving.

And then one day, she met a man who had dreams of moving to a new land where everyone was freer. He said the water was so fresh you could drink from the rivers and lakes, and the soil was so fertile anything grew.

At night you could see the stars. He was from a poor family and Hukyung's family disapproved at first, but he was quick-witted and the life of the party, and soon he won their hearts.

Eager to play with new pigments, she drew close to him. He said, 'Don't tell me any secrets. Whatever you can keep to yourself, do so.' That was the first clue. But they married and once they'd had three children, they decided to move. The idea was so beautiful that Hukyung could hardly contain the whirring of her muscles.

When they arrived she clapped her hands to her heart. The sky was so blue and wide, the air so fresh and fragrant. The ocean was near, and the hills, layered like rice cakes, were soft and delicious . . .

but they got used to it, and at home, before they moved, it had been black socks in a tub, and now again the soiled water overfilled and seeped through the house. She would hang the socks to dry but they would curl in like prodded beetles. She would darn the socks but every stitch undid another. She spent her days indoors, she was hardly allowed outdoors . . .

but when she could she swam and flew, her body collecting colours, dripping in pear tree green, east coast blue, kōwhai yellow to smear across a new canvas. She took her kids to the beach, made tiered cakes from sand, cored apples, told them folk tales . . .

until one day she fell deep into her trance and stayed longer and longer in her swan-state. The painting was clotted, the layers thick as blood. She had painted herself into her imagination. One side of her face was stuck, as were her splayed wings and stretched legs. All she could move was one eyeball: left, right, up, down.

Her children saw her absence as a migraine aura. The father had gone too, but the seasons took them under their circular arms. Rubbish trucks came and went, came and went.

*

Filial piety is a virtue of respecting and obeying and being devoted to one's elders. It is the basis of moral conduct and social harmony.

In the end, kindness is rewarded

or at the very least, remembered.

Those who once appeared clever are unmasked, the wind blows.

Do not be impressed by strong personalities, do not be fooled by the gloss of grandeur.

It takes time for the moral of the story to reveal itself.

*

One day, her youngest daughter was stopped in the street by a kea. It handed her something that looked like a big white seed, then flew away.

The daughter put the seed in her pocket and ambled home in the sunset. She began feeling something but was unable to articulate it. It grew in her—a moonbeam.

That night, when her flatmates were asleep, she ate the seed. It tasted like an old memory. She walked slowly around the house, waiting. At first there was nothing. She paced back and forth, bare feet cold on wood, and then she walked past a window and what she saw was unsurprising. It was clear.

둘

# The Taste of Home

도토리묵 / acorn jelly

The fluorescent lights guide me.

수제비 / flour balls

I fill the basket with ingredients,
not recipes, dropping a can here,
a packet there

김밥 / seaweed rice rolls

with no more thought than required
to continue forward, a simple
requirement, like delivering life-
changing news in a closed room.

물만두 / boiled dumplings

I wander the aisles, sneakers squeaking
with a sudden turn

순두부찌개 / soft tofu stew

to take in something just one more
time because

잡채 / sweet potato starch
noodles

it is hard to breathe when everything
is so beautiful.

김치찌개 / kimchi stew

I take after her in more ways than one
and when the time comes, I will laugh
at how I hated

떡볶이 / spicy rice cakes

to wait, how badly I wanted to be
gifted flowers.

된장찌개 / soybean paste stew

When I was younger, when I was
unwell, 엄마 would cook 된장찌개—
small cubes of tofu chipped at the
slightest of prods, potatoes danced freely
and the silverbeet slept.

미역국 / seaweed soup

These days, the taste of home interrupts.

짜장면 / black bean paste
noodles

Sometimes I wish I could return to bed
and see her open the door with one hand,
balancing a tray on one hip,

떡국 / rice cake soup

and when the time comes, all I will want
is 엄마's 된장찌개, but she won't be there
to comfort me

빈대떡 / mung bean pancake

because time is organised chronologically,
not thematically.

I see a man wave to a friend who doesn't
see him. The man does not persist, walks
off. I wonder if he will die before they can
meet again.

We line up at the checkout. Some move
faster than others.

된장찌개

And you will watch the conveyor belt
empty out.

It will come under one transaction.

And you will say thank you.

And the supermarket will close.

It all has to end somehow.

# Total Departure

is
the bit of pantyhose at the end, the bit my hand struggles to reach
a message that keeps trying to send, but we're deep in the bush
lodged in like pebbles in a sponge-lined pair of slides

it
sits still like the neighbour's cat, who watches from the driveway
with silver pins for eyes, only to run
when we get too close.

It is a mistake repeated enough times that
it becomes fate.
The rusting bonnet,
the soccer ball the kid across the road lost,
all buried in the blackberry bush.

We have driven off the road and into the blackberry bush
late at night, when
my flatmates are smudged into limbo
and the hallway is made of charcoal.

The last door is slightly ajar, is squiggled in grey
is omitting a baby's cry
is draped with a baby's hand
its little fingers curled
but I cannot enter so I turn and

in the window, leaning into
the night, I see her. Dressed in a long
white nightie, black stringy hair
to the waist, watching.
Slowly, smiling, she does the twist.

## A Part of Something

I'm yelling at the screen,
legs and arms flying out
like tarpaulin on a windy day.

Now I understand
what it's like to say 'us' instead of 'them',
to look up rules and rehearse them in my head
and feel the adrenaline rattle in.

My friend and I text.

At first we mimic the commentators, joking ('It's a three-point party!')
but soon we're speaking earnestly ('Can't believe he missed that lay-up')
and now, when someone asks how the game was,
I say, 'The Jets are a very emotional team, but with Hyrum out, it's not the same.'

I know what's going on.

There is a party but I am late, because the game is on.

I know competitive sports can and often do create and support
a toxic culture, especially in a male-dominated sport
such as basketball,
and I have read Brannavan's book about it,

but I am interested in the coaches
and how they design the plays.

I'm interested in how they, and the players,
make the most of every second—
how a time-out could be called in the last 20 seconds of the final quarter
and those 20 seconds could change the direction,

the outcome,
the legacy—

because now I understand the heart can make a technical foul:
unsportsmanlike behaviour that does not involve physical contact
but results in loss of possession, nonetheless.

Things could be planned to a T, the execution swift and precise,
all the players performing exact coincidences
and yet . . .

the digital scoreboard and timer sprint into new positions
no one could predict and now I understand

we are capable of hogging the ball,
dribbling it up to the free-throw line, leaping to dunk,
even though we know there is a real risk of missing the shot,
of letting our team down

but once you've built momentum, you're the star of the show baby!

And I'm a sucker for people who strive for excellence
in their chosen field, and universal templates that allow for surprises to occur
within the dynamics.

*The game's on bro, you watching?*

My boyfriend said each player's character is determined by
how clean they eat the chicken off the bones.

I crunch down on cartilage, suck the bones dry, but
my friend and I text and
I do not come to the party.

# Role Players

It was as he was playing NBA 2K20, the controller lit up like a mini spacecraft,
I thought about how there were a thousand different ways this could have
turned out.
With one or two specialised skills, play meaningful minutes, stay humble—
never complaining, performing dutifully, and it was when we kissed

I thought about how there were a thousand different ways this could have
turned out.
His mouth made me wonder about the mental hurdle of not being a superstar—
never complaining, performing dutifully, and it was when we kissed
there was a sudden blip, the lights signalling    through

his mouth    made me wonder about the mental hurdle of not being a superstar.
The room collapsed and
there was a sudden blip, the lights signalling    through
a time warp and

the room                    collapsed and
it was as he was playing 2K, the controller lit up like a mini spacecraft,
a time warp, and
with one or two specialised skills, play meaningful minutes, stay humble—

# Right Now, Wrong Then

Look closer:
little rats floating,
scrambling.

Tiny claws scratch blackboard heart.
The dam bursts.
The water rushes,

ripples vibrating
like an old Nokia on a bedside table
but now the rats have got the hang of it,

can stand on their boards,
are surfing
are frothing it

are laughing
wearing wraparound sunnies.
*Shaka*

The dam is about to flood the village,
like me.
Like me

the rats . . .
the rats are having
too much fun to realise.

# 80% of How Attractive You Are Is Determined by Your Haircut

At the hair salon you can choose a style
and rest easy knowing it will grow out.
Bubblegum pink, mullet, who cares, only you.
Like me, it could turn out
to be not what I imagined and        if it happens
I won't say anything        just book the next one
with someone else.

In school we wrote song lyrics on our hands and arms.
Often it took two or more showers to get rid of the tone.

We found it funny that words can be binding,
that we make promises we cannot know to keep.

At the salon they cut layers to mirror stages of trust,
modelled off a photograph of someone I admire.

We crack up loud, annoying
with our transparent plastic candy wrappers but

the awful truth is, for quite some time 'Accidentally in Love' from *Shrek 2*
has been one of my top-played songs on Spotify

and I think about one person like 90% of the time,
especially when dreaming in someone else's bed.

What is a relationship but    a bed of mussels
                                            a prominent feature of intertidal ecosystems?

*

Mussels live in shallow coastal waters, where they aggregate
into groups or clusters
formed by combining several similar elements
comprised of several species formerly regarded as
a single species and
taking the total score of a player or team in a fixture
comprising more than one game or round.

*

A monogamous relationship is one with two.

A polyamorous relationship is one where the couple have
other relationships too, that are both emotional and sexual.

An open relationship is one where the couple can independently have sex
with other people, but their emotional nest is with each other.

One type of polyamory is called a 'V' relationship—one person has
two relationships that hinge          like wishbones.

Another way to do it is to have a primary and secondary hierarchy.
You make the rules.
I am told there are as many configurations as there are people!

Sometimes I want to be in one of these versions because I trust how crazy we are
about          each other          I trust          there is no replacement
and only want us to make the most of being young and easy
on the eyes

but sometimes I feel it's somewhat forced, these rules
as if emotions could be     regulated
                    separate from
actions

using logic
and is it so bad to
                                        get caught in a
love

wearing the same clothes over and over again
until they                                                        rip?

Sustainability . . . of what?
and, re the baby problem, one word: community!

We have solved it all. Nothing is the matter.

Some say it's unnecessary risk, but I think we must be realistic
about at least one thing, and suppressing feelings
can manifest in dangerous ways like . . . throwing shit, also bruxism,
and what's wrong with approaching
people the way you do your wardrobe?

*

On a warm December evening my flatmates and I biked down
to the beach in togs, no shoes, towels over shoulders,
down the wide empty road, flat as a hand,
past houses set like solitaire rings and
I said, 'Would you rather have sex with someone you love
for the rest of your life, but you're always busting to poo,
or would you rather have sex with people you don't love
but you won't be busting?'

and Bex said, 'Someone I love'

and I said, 'What if you end up resenting them for always needing to poo,
what if it makes you not love them anymore?'

and they said, 'Well, that works both ways—they could feel bad about you
always needing to poo'

and I thought, *Clever Bex*

and the tyres rolled over the cooling road,
the sun slowly setting over us
like a dome of orange jelly,

but then Toby said, 'I would find someone who's into poo stuff, and love them'
and I thought, *Aha!* and said, 'True!'

Then Bex said, 'But you can't help who you fall in love with'
and it made me think of pheromones, and how Fergus had said,
'I'm never unsure about why I like someone, I'm never like
*Oh, it must be their smell*'

and how Hannah doesn't trust perfume because it covers pheromones
and how Campbell doesn't like perfume because it reminds him of relief teachers
and how I want to start becoming a perfume person because it's glamorous
also a handbag person     and . . .

*

Foolish consistency: When you insist on a conclusion for which the reasons are demonstrably false.

Heuristics: Because a rule of thumb serves to minimise risk and increase the likelihood of satisfaction.

Confirmation bias: The tendency to process information by looking for, or interpreting, information that is consistent with your existing beliefs.

*

Anyway I'm about attitudes, not topics . . .

and I wonder if I know how to love properly.
Sometimes I do worry, you know, about the quantity of it, like baking,
which I am so terrible at

but then I remember mussels are bivalves attached by means
of their strong byssal threads to a firm substrate,
staying, then detaching and reattaching
somewhere new.

The ocean washes over our bodies,
which rarely notice their own erosion.

Everything is ephemeral. We don't notice
the erosion of rocks much either, because
their lifespans are much longer than ours and

I don't want us to regret
or resent
I expect you to be absolutely honest about absolutely *everything.*
I know what I want.

I want us to last forever, like the walking dead.

Is that okay with you?

Oi, you there?

Text me back.

# Foraging

On long drives in the countryside, Mum would turn off whatever latest pop hits Cindy and I had tape-recorded and wind down all four windows. The car would suddenly balloon with air. We would seem to float around the bends, tilting towards the trees. The trees seemed so friendly, telling us they would catch us . . . and in this way we were gently bopped along, Mum sighing with happiness, homecoming. We grew tired of hearing the same story: *When we landed in New Zealand I could breathe!*

When we thought she might die, Mum and I hopped on a bus and went to a cabin at the top of a mountain in Korea. The cabin was in a small, rural town, close to the border, known for its military base and fresh air. She had already been back in Korea for a couple of years, and I had just arrived.

It was spring and the forest was thick. It was home to boars and snakes, so we wore heavy gumboots and carried small knives as we dug up root vegetables. Lunch and dinner were rice with yams, burdock, radish or lotus, blanched or steamed, seasoned with fermented soybean paste or soy sauce and sesame oil. We reached up to pluck pine needles and steeped them in hot water—I had read that this had saved sailors from scurvy. We were chasing any kind of remedy. I learnt to pick the dandelion leaves farthest from the road so our salads wouldn't contain exhaust fumes from farmers' trucks. We rested on big rocks, looked at things, the view. I tried to remember something about the sublime from my level 2 philosophy class to impress her but couldn't remember anything.

There were maybe ten wooden cabins perched on stilts throughout the uneven terrain, but we only met two other people. The landlady complained a lot and the sick man gave me the heebie-jeebies, because surely he would die any minute now. He had left the city for fresh air years ago, and that had bought him some time, but his family refused to join him or couldn't afford to, so he was all alone. I didn't want him latching on to *us*. I'd seen enough nature docos to know how this worked.

Every morning we walked down the mountain to the empty bus station and quiet buffet at the base. There was also a little shop, an old hanok, that sold military gear as souvenirs. The buffet was frozen in the past. Sometimes we'd stick around to eat in that empty room, stainless-steel chopsticks clanging against stainless-steel trays on the stainless-steel table. It was as if we were rehearsing for the hospital, or a percussion group with only the restaurant owner for an audience. Then we would walk back up the mountain. The mountain road was dry; very rarely would a truck drive past, kicking dust up into our faces.

Every afternoon we stripped down to our undies and camis and worked out to two YouTube videos: one cardio routine and one arm-strengthening routine. The doctor said it was important to do light exercise, and with the planned mastectomy she would need to develop shoulder muscles. I put the 11-inch laptop on the wooden table by the window and we clapped our hands, lunged from side to side, rotated our arms fast: 'Soccer Ball Arms'. This was followed by a shower. First she, then I, would crouch naked in the tiny tiled bathroom and pour buckets of cold water over thudding hearts.

I tried to think of it as a writer's residency—what a luxury to have whole days to write in isolation! But I didn't write. The loneliness was a heavy quilt; I kept falling asleep. The closest library was two bus rides away and the only books in English were a small collection of classics. I tried to get into *Middlemarch* but it wasn't my style. I was bored. She slept early and rose before the sun. I watched a lot of movies on the laptop, but I don't remember which ones. It all dissipated into a sick yellow cloud . . . That dust! It was so fucking dusty!

We were on the same mountain as the South Korean military training grounds, right by the DMZ. I went for runs in little shorts, past abandoned army tents in ditches, hoping to bump into a hot soldier. But run after run, empty roads. If only something exciting were to happen to me, I could be in a better mood for her. I didn't know how to cook anything proper; she made our meals. For her birthday I made a raw vegan blueberry cake but it was gross. She invited the landlady over to celebrate. I understood the sentiment and yeah it was her birthday, but I wished she hadn't.

We knitted fingerless gloves because it would be autumn soon. We made a poster locating the chakras because we felt desperate. There wasn't any glue so we mashed cooked grains of sticky rice between our thumbs and forefingers and tacked the coloured cut-outs onto black paper we'd found in the cupboard.

The only other thing is that I had a brilliant idea. A book about turtles, for children. I would write, Mum would draw. I needed twenty-four turtles. I hunted online for pictures of turtles from different angles. Watercolours and photographs, flippers stretched out and curved back, shells of various shades and patterns.

I covered the cabin in turtles I'd printed out at the internet cafe. I sharpened her pencils and propped cushions by the window, so she could sit comfortably and feel inspired by the sublime. *Draw a turtle!* I'd demand. I made a Pinterest mood board called 'Mum's turtles'. I put on a YouTube video and shoved it under her nose: *See how it drifts*. This could be the big art project she'd been saving herself for. I made her green tea so she could think in turtle colours. All she had to do was draw one turtle and then the rest would come easily. *Go on!* I cried from behind her as she stared at the blank piece of paper. *You're an artist!*

*Good idea, Eunsun*, she'd say, every time a new plan for the book came to mind. It would be published by Beatnik. Cindy could help with the design. Her grandkids would all be there at the launch, which would be held in an art gallery. Her paintings would be on display, too. She would get an artist's residency in Paris, like the one she gave up to be a good wife. Lots of rich and kind men would want to court her, and neither money nor loneliness would be a problem ever again.

But after a while, her shoulders slumped. *I'm tired*, she said. She hadn't drawn even one turtle. I took the turtles off the walls.

And one night, in the forest, a purple thunderstorm lit up the trees from behind.

The colour spread like a bruise from a gorse sting. We opened the big windows and lay on the bed facing the shadowed space, the pencilled ridge of the mountain, the black forest. It rained all night and the wooden floor got wet but it was warm. We stayed awake for as long as we could, searching for a sign.

Every third week we took the bus into Seoul and she spent three days in the hospital. I stayed at my aunt's.

The doctor said it was important to reward her after each bout of chemo, so after her first treatment I bought her a khaki-coloured bracelet woven from thread and adorned with a crystal turtle in the middle. Sometimes she told people it was the bracelet that was keeping her alive.

# Everything

Riverbanks, beige shoulders, touching.
Hands,
the tear-shaped clasp on the silver necklace.

Driving, stilling motion sickness.
The frozen corn cobs in plastic bags,
the hard-boiled eggs in plastic bags.

I can't escape,
nor do I want to.

Things that bounce: jumping, levers,
rolls of fabric.
Things that tire.

SPAM.
Checking the stitching, all over, twice.
Sets within sets, expectations, buffets.

Children, money,
holidays, houses.

Fun things, sad things.

Okay, okay yeah.

If not for the nudges it would all slide
like soap
away from the matter at hand.

셋

## They

are working on the brick apartment on the other side
of the office, floating above the street—
orange fish in an aquarium. We
lock eyes, the pierce of a hook. The water
wavers, my heart gasps—a pulled, lipless mouth—and I look away
and continue with administrative tasks, but the scaffolders are vivid
as a radiant heater. On sunny days
the window looks wobbly, like clear jelly I could swim through

and they

are there late into every afternoon. Their laughter filters through
silt, neon bodies glinting from the passing of steel tubes
and galvanised clips, from one side
of the clock to the other, building something. They sparkle
like a thousand dislodged scales and I wonder if we
could coordinate our movements, synchronise enough.
My daydreams bait me and catch me
and I dream of belonging in that school, in that part of the water

and they

are wearing bone hats and heavy boots but are weightless.
My colleagues and I sigh at the noise. Our annoyance ripples through
the glass but they don't notice or don't care, and
sometimes on my side of the glass it is perpetual summer.
Fish overheat, rise—a hard smear of silver. We
exist in the space of a fork pressed down into a baked day

and they

are muffled by repetition, but on rainy days

we notice their absence, the gap between two buildings now still water,
and we
are reminded of the way fish tails flicker only to disappear
through clouds, and I thought my side
of the glass was home, but sometimes I am a heavy piece of driftwood,
barely floating, and sometimes I am a shoe, caught in seaweed.
Don't get me wrong, sometimes I am a large rock . . .
Sometimes I am a set of perfect waves, rolling in at the pace
of fabric by the metre

and they,

they are long, flat mango seeds, swimming . . .

Today I arrived and saw them singing and dancing to Steps,
packing down after days, months, of building something,
and I suddenly felt a desperate need to be beside
familial gills, taking oxygen in the water
of our shared histories, but by the time I had shut down my computer
they were gone

but still I rushed to the window and threw
my body against the glass, smashing repeatedly with all my strength,
hoping the heat from the long days
would have decreased the glass's viscosity, so that the waters
could join, and what I mean is, sometimes I think about how we
will end up on our sides

in a sink, belly rising and falling.
How a knife pops the skin, quick as unpicking thread,
and how we only caught one side
of the reflection. When we're gutted, innards yanked out and
tossed to the dogs, you might not know that I spent a lot of my days
wishing I had learnt to swim in your part of the water.

## Someone Else's Dream

He teaches me how to ride a bike and that is one less fear.
I ride it to the gas station, him running beside me,

across bumpy roots and sunburnt grass, on the lake front
but I am not his wife.

We order pies and coffees and eat them on
the bench, looking out at pine trees. We do this often.

He shows me how to stand on the bike
and coast,

even and carefree but
I am not his wife.

Today I rode to the shop alone, got a pie and coffee
and the guy said, 'Is he resting today'

and the 'he' made me smile, the certainty and singularity of it
but I am not his wife.

# Its Body

stretches after one sleep. When freshly washed and dried it is taut and cool to the touch, but after the first night the middle pools. The corners remain as tight as brackets, but its body folds into small pleats, like a crowd of pursed lips. It is thin, nearing transparency, like the skin of a grape. It feels filmy and grimy, making it hard to grip. We roll in the ripples, pushing them further.

# Our Skin Rubs Off

A man goes to a bathhouse, and the ddaemiri scrubs his back with the ddaemiregae. She scrubs and scrubs, but dead skin keeps rubbing off. Finally, he admits he's an eraser!

*

She has a way of peeling fruit in one go. She holds the apple, pear or mango in one hand, wields a small knife with the other. She peels in a circular motion, starting at the core, until the skin of the fruit dangles in the sunlight, rotating slowly like a baby's mobile. When it catches the sun, it glows.

*

She is wearing my togs. Her sparse head of hair, like the top of a squashy doll's head, is dry. We are sitting in the shallow part of the pool. She is smiling sweetly, seeing shapes and colours—rhomboid tiles, old-swimming-pool blue—but I know something is off. I scan water-logged bodies. There is dirt in the tiles. The water is tepid. It is too quiet. Focus, tense.

In another dream she is wearing my black velvet headband, the one I wear before washing my face the way she taught me. She is lying on a couch in a library, wailing. The people look away, embarrassed.

In another, my friends and I are in an underwater mansion. She's there too. It's a party, but I'm distracted by her presence. I stand by her in the lounge, facing the wall-to-wall window, into the dark ocean, unsure what to do. But then two whales swim past—one is small, the other huge—and she grins and everything is okay, everything will be okay, because we've seen the whales.

*

A 때미리개 is a Korean exfoliating mitt. It's a square of coarse, sandpapery fabric with a wide opening for a hand to fit into. Every household has at least one—they're dirt cheap. Ours was the typical green with thin black strips near the opening.

In the shower, a few months into dating, I showed him how my skin rubs off. We faced each other in the small square. I rubbed my forearm with three fingers and put the skin in his hand.

*

The elders often discussed my shyness in front of me. I pretended I couldn't understand. They said I would shed this weak quality as I grew. We sat on silk cushions around low wooden tables.

*

I'm the friend who wants a baby. But if I have a baby, will the baby watch me be belittled? If I have a baby, will I depend on the baby? I don't want to depend on the baby, but I want a baby. If I have a baby, I will have to be sober for at least two years. Will I be able to say yes to the baby, yes you can sign up to the netball team, yes we can afford it. If I have a baby and the world is even more cooked, will I be able to say twenty years is better than none? If I have a baby and the baby is not healthy, is not happy, will I be able to love it enough? Will I be able to let it be, not try to change the baby to become more *my* baby?

*

She sits in the tub, submerged in steam, and calls for one of her daughters to scrub her back. The youngest comes in and assumes a low squat, one hand slipping into the 때미리개. The mother's back is turned. The water begins to shift with a rain of dead skin.

The flakes float in the water. They turn into tadpoles.

The mother feels lighter and lighter.

Suddenly, she realises she is being erased.

They are multiplying. They are hungry.

They assess the situation.

There is only one solution.

Don't watch.

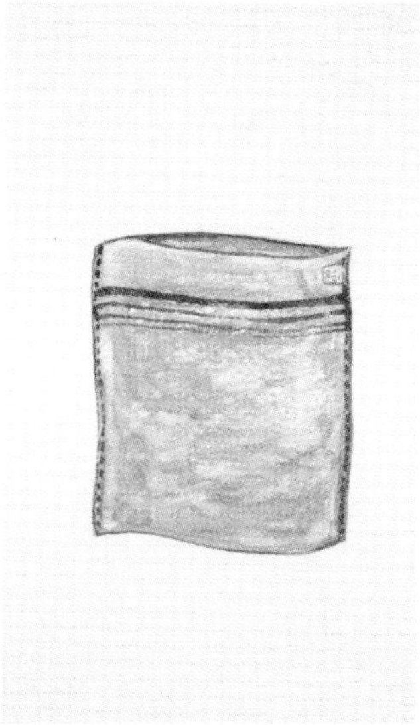

# IUD Removal

A lily—
its copper petals reaching . . .

the anthers
have been          pulled          off.

The root has burrowed
                                        deep
                                                        into fertile soil
and must be extracted in one scoop.
An earthquake is coming . . .
palm trees quivering . . .

In the distance a wind can be heard,
slow and wide at first, like someone walking
in bell-bottomed jeans,
then picking up
fast—

# When It Thinks It Is High Enough

The waves were tall, hitting irregularly. Two people were bobbing ahead, waiting for me to catch up, but from the rock face to my right I heard a continuous cry—something confused, or missing something, and I swam to the black rocks, leaving the others treading water.

When I reached the wall I saw a large bivalve, one shell ripped open, flesh exposed, beige and grey, slimy, wearing a pearl. It had no face but I knew it was crying but I also knew I couldn't understand it, didn't know how to comfort it. I held it a moment and then placed it back and swam away.

The sky becomes blue, the white clouds clapping clams, the surf bright and pulsing.

Back then, we foraged for seafood, using rocks to smash our way into oysters, rinsing them in the white swash; collecting buckets of mussels and cat's eyes and taking them home to crack open, to unfurl boiled bodies with toothpicks. Now we are able to remember what it tasted like.

On the shore a seagull flies up high, drops the shell that was in its mouth, picks it up, flies higher, drops it again. It keeps on doing this.

# Lasting Psychological Connectedness

See that house, down in the backyard?
Follow the wall of tangled jasmine.

She is cutting the heads of succulents
and preparing to replant them in pots,
trusting they will dig deep.

Chatty succulents spread gossip,
the way language began

and eventually, the stems will heal
and grow new roots.

The pots fret over their babies,
knitting moss sweaters, absorbing heat and water
and feeding them.

은선아, 날씨가 너무 더워. 잘 지내고 있어?

In the video of the birth
a hairy mound surfaces,
oozing . . .

## Pull Over, I'll Drive

I tried to be chill for you.
I started saying 'ya' instead of 'you',
sent texts without a second glance,
substituted baking soda for powder

and the banana loaf was a crowd favourite.
Baggy tees, sandy feet—
avocados went through as brown onions
and I started being late for meetings.

I tried to be chill for you,
leaving windows open at night,
taking one for the road,
letting the mail pile up till the snails got fat.

Cassette tapes, once unwound, are hard to rewind.
I tried to be chill, I really did.

I assembled 'tongue' and 'cheek' on the Scrabble board
before suggesting we go op shopping.

You never pitched in for gas but that was all good
cos money creates hierarchies,
accentuates the unimportant things

like shoes,
and you only liked that on the basketball courts.

My Spotify algorithms changed.
I started reading soft cover books in the bath.
The jug boiled and the water cooled.

I tried to be chill, for you and for me.
I tried to be chill,
but at the gig I scoped out the exit, just in case,
and you sculled your beer and turned
cos there was nothing left to say.

The next day we walked around town
and noticed the loop pedal at the busker's feet.

We got hungry.
We got food.

I knew these would be our last fish and chips.

So we ate in the park.
The sun went down.

## People Person

I'm trying to become more of a people person.
It's not easy when you gravitate towards netball,
a sport where a 90cm boundary between players
is clearly stated in the rulebook and, if you get too close, there is a penalty.

It's not easy when you like movies where not much happens, externally anyway,
or when sometimes you get so tired you feel
caught between overexplaining and saying nothing at all,
doing nothing at all because the things that matter are . . . . . .
but I'm trying.

I shake free gym passes—

'Come to the gym!' I urge.
They fly in the breeze like a high pony, not catching anything,
but I fool you into thinking I am a sporty person
because sporty people have the stamina to keep up

in group conversations, and the thing is, people people are also happy people
and even non-team exercise gives you endorphins . . . I have it all worked out . . .

In the garden, I have set up cones . . . I practise the beep test . . .

In school, I was always one of the last to be picked in PE
even when I was dating the team captain.

Now I know to never leave my fate in someone else's hands.

Now I can tell you the locations and closing times of Rebel Sports
and recommend a good running shoe (Asics GT-1000)
to take you along the denim coast.

My flatmate has started going for runs.
She told me she has to trick herself. When the thought
arises, she quickly puts on shorts and sneakers
and runs out the door before she realises what she's doing.

When I was little, 엄마 told me
sometimes we have to do things we don't want to do
and sometimes we want to do things but we shouldn't do them

but when I get shin splints I just keep running . . . and I run
to the pharmacy and instead of selling me compression tape
the person behind the counter says *Yeah so just stop . . .*
looking at me like I'm an idiot
but I am        and

sometimes I feel like a piece of tracing paper
sliding out askew, on top of the original image.

I feel like I'm driving a battered car through narrow streets
where there are loads of pedestrians and I am pushing
on the brake, wearing a very slippery bed sock . . .

The other night I was facing the wall, murmuring to myself
and he turned and snapped *What?*
and I said *Nothing, I was just murmuring to myself*
and he went *Why! You're not even doing anything!*

Sometimes fear flickers in his eyes
because sometimes my mind is not my own . . .
Sometimes I make sounds I have not heard before . . .
Sometimes I am                    Joanne . . .

and other times I am a blob of caramelised butter
on a stone plate,
simply unable to change in room temperature.

Sometimes I want to turn into a tampon and hide in my own
cosy vagina, where it is quiet . . .

Sometimes I feel like a sharp stone slab house built by the beach,
or a mesh mini on a winter night . . .

I have had an abortion but don't feel like writing about it . . .
I have been raped but don't feel like writing about it . . .
is that like having a Korean name and not using it?

Anyway I'm just saying, don't read too much into it.

Sometimes it's a game of bubble soccer—
adrenaline peaking, stitching laughter, but when it's over,
knuckles bloody from friction,
requiring a week to scab.

A people person lights up a room
with their summer asphalt heart.

A people person is not a leather couch.

A people person usually wins a staring contest.

On my wall there is a sheet of navy A1 paper.
The virtues of a people person are written in silver glitter gel pen.
Every day that I embody a virtue, I stick a gold star next to it.

Soon, my room will be a magnificent galaxy
and there will be a game of Duck, Duck, Goose
and the players will be stars
and I will be It, and I'll choose a Goose
and we'll run in circles, drawing loose constellations,
and I'll let myself be caught
and we'll collapse into the sparkles, like crystals on a velvet headband . . .

# The White Swans Are Dancing With Their Eyes Closed, In the Flurry

We play home design games on my phone. You peer over my shoulder as I click through various wallpapers, bedside tables and waterfalls for the turquoise pool. We take turns earning coins so we can keep decorating the multi-million-dollar mansion in the Caribbean.

People assume the houses I clean are like the mansions we decorate, but they're mostly the homes of young families where both parents are working full-time, or the elderly. They're usually empty when I arrive, but I've become so familiar with the things that fall off its inhabitants' bodies (hair, shit, jackets, crumbs) that I feel intimate and protective—an Egyptian plover in the crocodile's mouth.

When I was six, my parents worked as cleaners too. My brother's best friend's mum was also an employee, and when my dad realised he loved her more, he left. The next twelve years were a blur of clock hands: Mum stopped working and went on the dole, and we moved houses and/or schools every year. I became skilled at taking Blu-Tack off walls without ripping any paper; my sister was the best at durasealing books, rolling the plastic across slowly like clean waves, pushing them to break at the shore and then tucking them behind the cover. She and I tucked our hair behind our ears and walked together, across streets and parks, to all the new places.

Andrew is eight years older than me, five older than Cindy. When Dad left, Andrew got part-time work at an internet cafe, and for Christmas he got me a pink Barbie convertible, Cindy a Mulan doll, and Mum a bottle of Forever and Ever Dior. Days before, Cindy and I watched as he sprayed the bottoms of his school shoes with a can of fake snow and stamped footprints on the back steps. I don't remember the actual day but it's the first Christmas season I remember. There are kaleidoscopic flashes of silver on the card, which Andrew signed 'from Santa C'—our surname still being 'Cho', as by Korean law we were still Dad's.

In the months we stayed at Dad's, Andrew drove us to school in his ladybug-blue Mazda, sharing his music and jokes. He and Cindy were at the high school and intermediate school neighbouring each other, but my primary school was on the other side of the hill. They often got detentions for being late, catering to my later start. They couldn't say the truth, because Andrew was on his learner's. When we drove over the harbour bridge on a sunny day and there was a big truck in the next lane, Andrew made a game of driving parallel to it so we'd be in the shade. We loved him for these things and also because before that,

a few months after our parents split, Mum entered a competition at the local Korean health store and won plane tickets. We were moving back to Seoul. Andrew was to stay behind with our Kendo teacher's family to finish his term at school and join us a few months later. And it's because that night, waiting for us to leave him in the airport lounge, he saw me slouched on the chair all grumpy because Cindy had gone to the souvenir shop with the coins she'd saved up and got herself a gold-plated kiwi statue, but I didn't have any money and it was late and there was too much waiting, and he suddenly appeared crouched at my side, dangling a silver charm bracelet with all these lovely leaping dolphins and clasped it around my wrist.

So we did return to our own country. The sounds, the lights, were all harsh, and the unpredictability rolled me; I wet the bed a lot. There was no grass, and I hid in the toilets during lunch even though Cindy told me that the kids who were chasing me were only shouting 'Say something in English!' because they wanted to be my friend. I went to two schools. At the first one I had a great teacher who sat me at the front of the class and taught me the alphabet; at the second one I had a teacher who beat up a kid in front of us, smashing her head against the door and so on, and Mum says that's the day I came home and cried, sat in her lap and asked her to send me back home. She says a light came on and that's when she decided we'd all move back, she realised she hadn't seen me laugh happily once while there but

I remember Mum taking us to the clothing warehouse, hunting for clothes so she could sell them for more, and Cindy and I would spend hours playing on a mountain of sequins and velvet and diamantés and lace. I remember bus trips to the beaches and relatives we'd never met, Cindy and I clutching our matching soft toy dogs, eating jelly drinks and snacks with cartoon characters on them; the stationery shops by the schools where we loitered, flicking through racks of stickers and trays of coloured card; the empty apartment the landlord let us be witches and doctors and ballerinas in; sprinting home to beg Mum for some baby chicks a man was selling from a cardboard box outside the school gate; roasted chestnuts wrapped in newspaper, fish cake on skewers in a paper cup filled with broth; the spiky green and black fake hair bun Cindy and I took turns wearing, only taking it off at the bath house . . .

and Andrew arrived and surprised me at school. I jumped up into his arms, legs strapped around his waist and the kids said, 'Is that your dad?' Andrew made us laugh but we took him in a train to his boarding school in another city. It didn't matter though—Mum remembered the reasons why she'd left Korea in the first place, and a few months later we were at a motel in Auckland called 'Cho's Motel'.

Andrew didn't always live with us, but Cindy and I were two flowers from the same stem. Mum made us variations of the same outfits. In one photo we are sitting on the couch in matching red corduroy dresses, the only difference being mine has big black pockets—she is frowning, I have a toothy grin, proud. We put on fashion shows, practised dance routines, all curated by her. Oh my god, my siblings were so good at dancing, had so much charisma, I don't know how they didn't become famous. When we lived at Dad's, it was Cindy who made sure I brushed my teeth, asked me how my day at school had been, told the homestay kids off when they teased me. I remember the challenge of taking a raw egg home from school, keeping it alive until the next day.

We loved to play pretend. My favourite persona was 'fishmonger'—I would put one hand in a plastic bag, crawl around picking up toys and then quickly invert it and tie it up like they did at the fish market. We made obstacle courses, jumping across furniture, competing for the quickest time. We sewed for our dolls—a tiny pillow stuffed with blonde hair brushed from their heads, a wedding dress from Andrew's white boxers—and had mailboxes tacked to our bedroom doors for the notes and letters we wrote to each other. Sometimes she used her special stamp to sign off—a blue tweety bird. We were scared of going to the toilet by ourselves, so we always went together, one climbing the corridor walls while the other peed in between fits of laughter.

When we were a bit older, it was Andrew who came to my parent teacher interviews after an all-nighter shift at the hotel; it was Andrew who used his pay to shout us to our first BurgerFuel dinner; it was Cindy who wrote out my class presentation in her neat hand because I couldn't print it out; Cindy who, after I'd been ball dress shopping with some of my wealthier friends, said she'd help me make one—we sewed a minidress with off-cut linen and stitched a tiered skirt with dried-out tea bags that were stained pink, and bordered the high waist with sequins. The whole fit, including the gold heels we found at an op shop, cost $26.

These are the narratives we tell over and over again; they keep us connected through all the distance we have created and maintained. Our relationships shrink and expand and shrink again like a jellyfish opening and closing its bell. Blood tethers, clots.

Our true reactions and preferences are inconsistent, but we smooth these out by reframing our experiences in a consistent narrative.

We are good at keeping secrets from each other, our bodies an advent calendar—occasionally one of the little flaps opens and a piece of chocolate falls out.

Each version of the family stories forms an overlapping polyphony. These are our heirlooms and we are the school choir.

As I got older it became harder to weed my garden, I didn't have the right tools, and for a while I could see no other flower heads. Andrew and Cindy moved out, had families of their own. Mum and I closed our doors and then opened them only to slam them shut. We had piles of old copies of *Vogue* we bought for 50 cents at the Sunday market, and we flicked through them in silence. Occasionally I'd wave a page at her and say, 'I like this,' and she'd say, 'No,' and then later she would point her finger at something and I'd tell her that her pick was bad too, even if sometimes I disagreed with myself.

I don't know a lot of Korean. We don't speak the same language, but I am my mother's daughter. We have the same tongue, sometimes sharp like cutty grass, sometimes soft as Lamb's-ear. Sometimes we are as strong and jubilant as a bouncy castle, and other times we are like slow-cooked pork falling off the bones in gamja-tang.

*

Mum says we moved so often because she didn't feel settled; she was scared. We mainly lived on the North Shore because there was a large Korean community there and because she thought it a good neighbourhood. When we first immigrated, in 1995, Mum wanted to take English lessons but he wouldn't let her. He said he would learn and speak for them both. She says he trained her to be a good housewife and didn't like her leaving the house or socialising without him.

She says she was his rice: someone who is easy. When he left, he simply said he didn't know things would happen this way, that she should accept it as fate. Then she tried to learn English but the sounds wouldn't enter her ears, she just sat at the desk, tears streaming down her face.

She joined the Korean Catholic church because some of her friends went there, and when she began reading the Bible she was surprised by how similar the teachings were to the Buddhist teachings she'd been brought up on. She called it a quiet religion, and when I asked her how she could switch so easily from one belief to another she said she didn't believe in the existence of one religion. I said I understood: that that's how I felt about romantic relationships. She said she wished I would go to church with her.

A couple years ago I went to therapy for the first time. It was your idea. Therapy was 90% more expensive than meds, but once I signed up I was informed I was eligible for a year's worth for free. I went studiously, taking notes after each session. Sometimes she wanted me to talk about things I felt I'd moved on from and I felt like I was sitting a test, failing to deliver the desired results. Sometimes I was amazed at how she could make me arrive, using a route I hadn't thought of. She taught me to pay close attention to how my body tries to fight or fly, and how I could take a breath, a moment, and choose how to respond. You can calm your body and mind by repeating simple phrases like 'I'm safe' and 'I deserve to be here'. Sometimes I felt so silly I'd laugh until I cried. Afterwards Jonty would come over for wines and I'd be like, 'Do you think she likes me?'

*

Mum has started looking forward to things. She's been getting into star charts and has discovered that 65+ is when she'll be blessed with the most luck. The last time I visited her my vision was blurring from a late night and I had a large takeaway coffee in my hands. For the past three years she's been in a shared living situation—it used to be a commune that got busted for manufacturing drugs and for sexual assault. I don't know if she knows that. *She* moved into an eco-village. There's around a hundred people, each with their own rooms and shared kitchens and bathrooms.

Her room is upstairs, in one of the wooden houses dotted in the forest. It is small, cosy, cluttered. Small cuts of paper are tacked to the walls with sketches and paintings. She has travel-sized bottles of homemade lotions, an easel facing a Swiss ball, a photo of herself with shoulder-length hair, a mound of mandarins and lemons, a thermos, a face massaging tool, and small scraps of hemmed cloth under everything. For curtains, she has pinned up two pieces of rectangular, cream-coloured knits using gold tacks and fishing line.

The bed is centred against the front wall, by the door. Above it is a long piece of floral fabric with a scalloped edge, tacked up like a headboard. On the clothes rack is a brown oilskin jacket, a long blue-and-white striped skirt with silver threading, a cashmere sweater—she has a superpower for finding gems in op shops and never paying more than $10. But also, multiplying like cells: fistfuls of blunt pencils in jars, random wall hangings (dulled ribbons, calendars from every church, a forest fairy), porcelain figurines with melting faces, a rusty lamp that she's decorated with broken earrings and rhinestones . . . I wonder if it's so that when she dies, which she predicts will happen in five years, there is something for us to pick at, like seagulls by the bay, pecking at rotting remains. And on the bed, in between a bundle of soft toys and cushions, is a swan-shaped pillow: white plumage, curved, elongated neck. A side profile. It has one closed eyelid lined with long, black lashes, and on its head is a sparkling gold crown. It looks happy.

On the day I visited she also had two crystal wine glasses, because she thought I was going to stay with her, in her bed, and thought we would get a little tipsy and share stories.

Instead I had decided to stay at a friend's in town so I could party until the street-cleaners drove in. When I visit I'm usually only in town for the weekend and I'm hungover for half of it, and she puts on lipstick and smiles wide, wanting to be her best for me, her gold back teeth sparkling. I sank onto her bed, still clutching the cup of coffee as she paced her room, gesturing, eyes darting: 'I wake up and open the windows to hear the sound of the stream . . . Sometimes I catch myself in the mirror and I'm smiling! And it's so funny that I'm smiling—I'm just in my room by myself! But I'm laughing all the time now. Sometimes I feel like I'm living in a dream! How did I get so lucky!' She wiggles slightly whenever she's excited. Her small frame washed across me—the ticker on a metronome.

She stopped pacing and perched on the edge of the bed, tentatively. She patted the wool blanket that covered the lower third of the bed. She looked me in the eyes and smiled. I took a sip of coffee. 'I got a tattoo of my friend's name,' I said, jutting out my elbow. Her smile didn't wane. She said, 'It's nice to have a soulmate.' I put my arm down and sighed.

Through all the moving, the one thing Mum kept were her jewels: a thick gold chain set with a bevelled sapphire; diamond chandelier earrings; a slim leather watch, its face lined in iridescent opal; rings topped with rubies and emeralds; a crystal choker. These were heirlooms from her ancestors and she planned on passing them down to my brother's wife, my sister and me. She loved dressing up and being ID'd at the supermarket. She wore the woollen cardigan and vest Armani set, in stripes of brown and cream, the black nylon Prada bag, the reversible Burberry waterproof hat—all the designer clothes from her youth she made last. The only time she didn't wear jewels was when she went to her monthly WINZ appointments. This was because once someone working there told her to sell her jewels, to return to her own country, and cut off her benefit. When things like that happened we were lucky to have a friend offer help, but slowly, everyone stopped visiting.

I remember her unclasping a bracelet—I sat at the bus stop, holding it carefully in both hands, legs dangling, waiting for her to emerge from the automatic doors.

*

In high school I made Mum a CV and bullied her into coming with me to a wanky clothing store because she'd worked in fashion in Korea. The elderly white woman was dressed all in black, with manicured nails and chunky silver rings. She looked Mum up and down and said, 'Do you have experience?' and then to me, 'Does she speak English?' I avoided looking at Mum but could feel her sinking beside me. I didn't push her again, but years later I made her drive to vineyards with her paintings, because she'd been a promising painter too.

When I turned eighteen Mum didn't qualify for the solo parent benefit anymore, and I didn't want to live with her, so she moved back to Korea and found work as a caregiver at 꽃동네, meaning 'Flower Village'. This is a huge centre in a large forest. People used to abandon babies with disabilities in the bushes, propped them up against tree trunks. They were rescued by the workers and named after the plant they were found by, and given the surname of the priest who founded the place ('Oh') for they were all his children. Due to DNA tracing this happens less often now, but women rescued from gangs are still brought here. Some of the women have been raped, tortured, made to beg on the streets; the women are unwanted for having mental or physical disabilities. Mum worked in the women's department. The women were rated on a scale of 1–10 in terms of their severity. Mum worked with the 8–10.

I went to visit once. Mum and the other workers bunked in shared rooms, but when I was there she got a hotel room for us. It was so luxe it hurt. It angered me. She said my anger reminded her of him. She took me to work one day. There was shit and period blood smeared across the walls. There was wailing and silence.

One of the women had been raised in Russia, by a Russian mother and Korean father, until her mother died and her father didn't want to take care of her anymore. He sent her here, to a new country where she didn't understand the language or the food. She didn't speak words they understood, neither Russian nor Korean, but my mum seemed to understand her sounds. Mum became the only person who could reassure her. When she couldn't, the wards strapped the woman down and injected something. This made Mum really sad.

I stayed two nights and then left her.

Now, Mum is back in Auckland and has casual cleaning jobs, but her main part-time job is to drive to elderly women's homes and wash them, give them their pills, cook things she's never cooked before: baked beans and sausages on toast. Her eyes widen with glee as she tells me about one client who has high cholesterol but insists on eating bacon. She finds it funny, their habits and attachments. Some of her clients refuse to talk to her, turning up their nose, yelling commands from across the room, and I wonder if they know who she is—the mythical swan maiden, the princess of the Moon family, the prodigy of the fine arts department. 'Show them your powers!' I want to yell.

But she's become close to the others, massaging their hands and telling them they're beautiful. She tells me that older people living alone miss being touched. She tells me to listen to their stories. On Wednesdays I clean for an elderly woman—this is the only client who is home when I am. Her husband has died and she is slowly cleaning out his stuff, but his muddy gumboots still stand by the back door. They are the one thing she can't get rid of. I go early and have a cup of tea and shortbread, and ask her to tell me how they met, about their long life together. On the phone I hear her refer to me as 'the cleaner'. I practise putting that aside, practise hugging tight.

When I was thirteen, one of Mum's brothers died and she collapsed outside my room, still clutching the phone. I sat there at my desk, watching her fall apart. After a long time she said, 'Can you please hold me.' I was alarmed that that hadn't occurred to me naturally.

*

Closure isn't a one-off conversation or activity, it's an ongoing process that requires not just time but active work. So we grate the potatoes, skin and all, slap them into patties, fry them, fill the plate, feed the family, keeping it moving.

*

You're my best friend and you've just scored an office job so now you're saving to buy a house. Or land. I don't earn enough to save, but I'm in on the plan. It's called an investment. You're investing in me, and I in you. Capitalist language for survival's sake. The plan itself is hazy but at the centre is my mum. We'll have a big garden and sign onto one of those tiny home schemes; she can live with us but still have her own space. We talk about building a life together. We watch YouTube videos of people building houses out of mud. Why couldn't we do that? There's heaps of mud around here.

Sometimes, if I think about us breaking up, I feel like I'm letting my mum down. I sleep best when burrowed between your shoulder blades, warming my face with your heat. True confidence in a relationship is not buying copies of your favourite books because you can just read their copies, but I can't shake this feeling that I'm using your resources without contributing my fair share.

When I was little and had a sore tummy Mum would lay me on her lap, rub slow circles on my stomach and sing, 'Eunsun's stomach is a poo stomach, Mum's hand is a medicine hand.' There was another song too.

It went like this: 'Eunsun has become Mum's prisoner of war!' and then she'd grab me and tickle me and I'd scream and laugh and try to fight her off. I remember how taken care of I felt when she'd brush my hair in a way that didn't hurt. Her long plum cardigan with the pointy buttons, it always smelled of roses, and that smell would comfort me and haunt me.

Now, when you're gone, for days or weeks, playing basketball, I miss the smell of Kawakawa ointment, the pharmacy aftershave, smells of a million people, but I can only associate them with you. I wear your hoodie, tying the drawstrings tight beneath my chin, unsure when it stops smelling like you, becomes me. The smell of arnica at night when you rub it thick into your thighs before jumping into bed. The smell of chamomile tea. We prescribe order to what we can control, meditating on the sweet lulls of repetition, riding the waves. They send us to sleep.

When you had night terrors and bolted out of bed and began sprinting up and down the stairs outside our room, that was crack-up. I was still awake. I asked what you were doing. You freaked out, couldn't stop running. I tackled you to the floor, locked you between my thighs, used my free arm to grab my phone. Put on the NBA highlights. You relaxed immediately. This is intimacy.

Being in love and being loved back is like losing something and coming across it much later, in a stranger's flat. We've built a foundation, we're going to build a house—but one natural disaster and even a house you own isn't yours anymore. We watch things crumble, break into smaller and smaller pieces until they are no longer substantial enough to be called what they were originally, but we cling on anyway. We drive to the houses we used to live in just to stare, even though they've completely changed and only the walnut tree is recognisable. Still, I ask if you want a photo in front of it and you say yes, pose.

I've moved around a lot and now I want to just hang out for a bit, take care of myself, blue skies, blue seas.

I don't know the measurements or materials, which way it will face or the design, but in my mind there are green fields, the summer glow like popping candy, and it's just me, spinning in honey-scented alyssum and burst fig, and there's the river, there's the tin fishing boat, the friendly trees, and I am spinning and spinning and when I fall I look around and it looks a bit like

Blenheim?

When I call, she picks up quickly.

Oh Eunsun, I wanted to tell you something—

Yes?

Yesterday I thought every worry from the past, everything unsolved, suddenly is no longer a problem.

That's good.

I was walking along the beach and I suddenly realised it's all okay, I've had thoughts like this before but it would come and go, I would dwell on the past again, but this time this feeling came back and back again and again and I was walking down the beach laughing to myself.

That's good. So you're well?

Yes, I'm good. When I moved back five years ago, the doctor said if I made it past five years I would be okay, but I honestly didn't think I would make it but now it's been six years and I can feel my body is stronger, I can move my arm a lot, truthfully my insides aren't so great but I think I will live the rest of my life like this, getting a little lump removed now and again, it's not like I'm going to die right now, I think I will plan my life in five-year increments. I have five years left. I want to travel.

Do you want to go to Australia?

No, I want to go to Fox Glacier.

Ah, good.

I want to go in winter, I love the cold . . .

Yeah good, do you mind if I help you research?

Yes! Find out for me. How to get there, where to stay. When I went twenty years ago I stayed at a youth hostel and it had a spa, it really helped me with the cold.

Don't stay at a hostel, I'll find you a cheap motel or something. I can help.

No, I don't need help, I have so much money!

Me too! I've got $1000!

I don't plan on saving to buy a house, I spend all my money on living my life.

I thought you wanted a house, last time we spoke—

No, I changed my mind, I don't want to be tied down. Having money is so stressful.

Yeah.

But don't forget I still have the jewels for you!

I don't want them, I won't wear them.

Then sell them and keep the money.

No, just keep them or give them to someone else.

I'll hold on to them until you want them.

I don't want them!

Your children might want them.

I don't know if I'll have children.

Okay, okay, I'll hold on to them for you. Oh, Eunsun, I want to be free! I want to do everything I want to do in the next five years.

Okay, I'll look up Franz Josef and plan it. Tell me what else you want to do and I'll look into those too.

Yeah, do that. If I was going with another person it'd be nice to rent a car and drive around . . . But it looks like it'll be just me so keep it easy, just one location.

Okay, I'll look into it.

*Pause*

What did you do today?

Ah, I cleaned the Korean grandmother's home, I didn't last week because I was with Haeyoung. And I've just had lunch and am in my room . . .

Okay, okay, well I'll look into Franz Josef and text you.

Okay, thanks for calling. I love you *very* much.

Yeah, I love you too Mum.

# Notes

'Send to Robyn Immediately' is taken from the song title 'Send to Robin Immediately' by Robyn.

The basketball documentary in 'A Winning Attitude' is *The Last Dance* by Jason Hehir.

In 'Role Players' I recycled the explanation of a role player from Hoops Addict: hoopsaddict.com/what-does-a-role-player-mean-in-basketball/

In 'A Part of Something', Hyrum is Hyrum Harris from the Manawatu Jets 2020 team. I also reference Brannavan Gnanalingam's book *Sprigs*.

'Right Now, Wrong Then' is the translated title of a movie directed by 홍상수 (Hong Sang Soo).

The eraser story in 'Our Skin Rubs Off' is from a joke in a late 90s Korean comic I can't remember the name of.

The title 'When It Thinks It Is High Enough' is taken from the clip 'How do seagulls crack a shell?' from New Atlantis WILD: youtube.com/watch?v=AcHvpoD59Aw

Some of this work has been previously published in slightly different forms in *Hainamana*, *Somewhere a Cleaner*, *The Spinoff*, *Stasis*, and *Sweet Mammalian*. Thank you to the editors.

# Acknowledgements

Thank you to:

Mum for the illustrations, for supporting and trusting me to write about you, and for being my mum!

Josiah Laracy for being a consequential muse, and for your support.

The MA class of 2020 for your guidance and generosity, for keeping the fever high: convenors James Brown and Anahera Gildea, classmates Safia Archer, Sarah Catherall, Areez Katki, Joan Skinner, Barbara Sumner, Ethan Te Ora, Justine Whitfield and especially Fergus Porteous for workshopping every version of this and encouraging me right till the end, for being my sounding board.

Madison Hamill and Olly Clifton for your feedback and conversations.

Annaliese Brown and Cindy Cho for reading earlier versions of this, and Jonty Buchan for being my first reader and the first person I call.

All the people I derived content and inspiration from, including but not limited to Hannah Bridger, Oliver Buchanan, Harriet Campbell, Andrew Cho, Toby Edgar, Bex McKenzie, Ella Rudin, Campbell Stonehouse.

Te Herenga Waka University Press, in particular Ashleigh Young, for turning this into a book.

Pip Adam for the kind words.

Constance Mary for the cover photos; the Wynne family for the location.

Axel Olsthoorn for the cover design.

Finnley Meekma and Hana Thomson for your enthusiasm and all the misc. help.

The Friends of Robert Lord Writers Cottage and UBS Dunedin for letting me stay at the Cottage to write, and my colleagues at Playmarket for having my back during this time.

Everyone else who's been around . . . Thank you for indulging me in this! Feeling blessed. Lots of love and gratitude.